Finding
Joy
Again

AMMIE BOUWMAN

*A Manual for a
Joy-Filled Life*

Published in the United States by Credo House Publishers,
a division of Credo Communications, LLC, Grand Rapids, Michigan
credohousepublishers.com

Unless otherwise noted, Scripture quotations are from the Holy Bible,
New International Version®, NIV® Copyright ©1973, 1978, 1984, 2011
by Biblica, Inc.®. Used by permission. All rights reserved worldwide.

ISBN: 978-1-62586-155-9

Cover and interior design by Frank Gutbrod
Editing by Donna Huisjen

Printed in the United States of America
First edition

Dedicated to Marj Newhouse:
who had a dream to help those battling depression and
asked the question "Would you like to teach a class?"
My answer and God's prompting changed everything!

"As the Father has loved me, so have I loved you.
Now remain in my love. If you keep my commands,
you will remain in my love, just as I have kept my
Father's commands and remain in his love.
I have told you this so that my joy may be in you
and that your joy may be complete."

—JOHN 15:9–11

Contents

Introduction *1*

Chapter 1 Detours and Disappointments *5*

Diving Deeper *15*

Chapter 2 Rebuilding Our Foundation on the Word,

Not the World *21*

Diving Deeper *31*

Chapter 3 Putting on the Full Armor of God,

Because It's a Battle *37*

Diving Deeper *49*

Chapter 4 Replacing the Lies with the Truth *55*

Diving Deeper *65*

Chapter 5 Faith and Hope Bring Joy *71*

Diving Deeper *81*

Chapter 6 Daughter, Your Faith Has Healed You *87*

Diving Deeper *99*

Chapter 7 Find the JOY *105*

Diving Deeper *117*

Acknowledgments *123*

Notes *124*

Introduction

I spent the first three-quarters of my life trying to make a good first impression. Those first thirty seconds were imperative for me. I needed that person I encountered to believe that I was healthy. Believe that I was perfect. Believe that I had it altogether. Believe that I was happy. I had developed a technique of transforming my face, lifting my eyes, and brightening my smile—just from the sound of footsteps or a shadow passing by. I had perfected the sound of my voice, lifting the end of the sentence to a higher octave and incorporating the right amount of sincerity at a moment's notice.

"I'm good, how are *you*?" Sometimes the phrase would hang in the room while the person passed by, just a wave of acknowledgment and a "good" as they went about their day. But sometimes they would stop to answer the hanging question. When they did, I was attentive, easy to talk to, and consistent. If you were to look up a "good listener" in the Cambridge English Dictionary, there would be a snapshot of my face with the label "Perfection." And when they would walk away, they would never know that I had a mental illness. They would never know that I felt unhappy, unloved, and somehow disappointed with how my life was turning out.

It's amazing when you condition yourself to make that first good impression how it stays with you like a fabric softener, always ending up sticking to some part of you that you can't see. It's a mentality that carries over into other areas of your life. It's no longer enough to just make a good first impression; you need to be the most attentive mother, the perfect wife, the most reliable and dependable employee, and the BEST friend. And every area of your life needs to look perfect. I mean, What if someone were to come over? My house needs to be clean. What if I were to run into someone I know? I'd better look good. What if, What if, What if? And all the while you're exhausted and lonely, living your life inside four glass walls with an uncontrollable thirst for acceptance, peace, and joy.

So my question for you today is Are you happy? Are you walking around in an "I'm Fine" shirt, pretending that everything is okay but all the while suffering in silence as you battle depression, anxiety, hopelessness, and feeling that you'll never experience true joy? Well, if that's you, I'm so glad you found this book. God is reaching out to you, letting you know that He has great plans for you and wants you to have His joy, the kind of joy that only He can give you. The kind of joy that doesn't come with things we purchase, dreams we chase, houses we live in, and lies we believe about ourselves. True joy comes from the Father, who created us. I know because I've been there. I've traveled my own journey searching for happiness. I have had to strip off the layers of this world that I have collected over my 49 years and find that little girl inside me, the one who knew who she was and knew that God loved her unconditionally. I've had to rebuild my foundation of beliefs, identify the break in my life where I started to believe the lies from the enemy, lay down those suitcases filled with lies, and replace those lies with the truth. And when I did that, I did find my joy again. It's possible. It's so possible that you can reach out and grab it. You just need the tools. You just need to believe.

So won't you join me? Let's start a journey of truth, stepping toward who we truly are in Christ and what it looks like to follow Him. And as you turn the pages, just take His hand. He is walking with you. He will help you find your joy again . . .

Ammie Bouwman

CHAPTER 1

Detours and Disappointments

When we think about beauty, we have our own image of what that means. It could be the sun dipping into the evening sky, leaving a trail of color as though it were painted by the very hand of God. It could be the first moments a baby enters the world, crying out for its mother and quieting when she finally hears her voice for the first time and settles into the crook of her neck. Or it could be seeing a person helping a stranger; watching them give a steaming cup of coffee into trembling hands and relishing the smile form as that stranger feels love, maybe for the first time in a long time.

However you view beauty, the definition has become a part of you, and you use that word along a sliding scale in your everyday life. We rate the sunsets each day, the people we work with, the images of the men and women on the magazines at the checkout, and the way we see ourselves. Somehow we have gathered that word and what it means to us into our arsenal of feelings and beliefs, and we use them as part of our foundation of who we are. And we not only rate "beauty" but compare. I'm not sure this is a tendency we're born with, but it's definitely something we're taught as we live in this world. *I'm not as beautiful as X, but I'm definitely more beautiful than Y. And don't even get me started on Z. She could really use some beau-ti-fi-ca-tion.*

Have you ever said something like that? I'll admit that I have. I've rated and weighed and measured my whole life, and all the while I was looking only at the outside of someone else—not to mention myself. I had my "definition," and if she didn't fit neatly into the box of what I thought beautiful was—if she didn't fit the right dress size or wear the right hairstyle, or if she shopped in her pajamas, I wouldn't let her into my circle. I knew what I needed to keep my world turning in the right direction, and I kept to that orbit, for better or worse.

But where did that insane thinking come from? I don't think it was taught in pre-k. I don't think I woke up one morning and everything looked different. Or maybe it did. Let's take a moment and imagine a young girl sitting on her bike (you know, the one with the banana seat and the fringes on the handlebars), ready to take on the world. She has a carefree smile and courageous demeanor, and her only concern is where she will go next. She had her mom gather her hair into two ponytails and then raced out the door, ready to take on her next adventure. She didn't care what anyone thought, what her dress size was, or whether she and her mom shopped in their pajamas. She fully embraced her tomboy ways and knew without a doubt who she was and that the Lord loved her unconditionally.

I loved this girl! I loved her outlook, the way she looked at people, the way she looked at herself. She was confident of who she was, and her foundation was built on the Lord. She had so much JOY! So what happened to her? She grew up. The world broke in and revealed to her that people fall out of love, marriages end, people change, and words can hurt. And with the closing of one door, another one cracked open, allowing the enemy of her soul to whisper lies about who she was and what her orbit should be. She started caring about her appearance, what the scale said, and what people said about her, and she doubted that the Lord could really love her after everything she had done. Her whole world started to revolve around something else, around who she "needed" to be.

You see, the girl in the ponytails, with the fringes on her handlebars and the wind in her hair, was me. My life took a drastic turn in 1981 when my parents divorced, leaving me unsure of my place in the world. While I still loved the Lord, I had buried pieces of myself in the backyard of my heart and built tall walls around who I was. I needed to self-preserve. I needed to guard my heart. I needed to rely on myself.

Is this what happens? Is this how our definition of beauty is created? Is this how our foundation is formed? I know that it is. At 11 years old I didn't stop what I was doing, put all my emotions on hold, go to the Word, and read Psalm 139:13, "For you created my inmost being; you knit me together in my mother's womb." As my parents were getting a divorce I was thinking "This is my fault!" My foundation, which had been built on God and my family, began to crumble, and I was no longer confident in who I was but believed that I had been a mistake. They'd had to get married and have me. I hadn't been planned. And I was now the reason they were getting a divorce. That door that cracked open on my broken foundation now allowed the enemy access, and as he began to tell me every lie about who I needed to be and what that would look like, I drifted farther away from who I was and how God had designed me to be. My world, like so many other people's, became conditional, and the certainty of the true beauty that lies within us, painted by the hand of God, nurturing the souls of the infants we are and loving us with unconditional love, without judgment, and looking past all of the reasons we're standing there right now with trembling hands, was replaced by the image of a sliding scale.

I became fixated on myself and what I knew I needed to do to remedy my deficiencies. My caring heart and courageous demeanor became guarded, and I started to worry about where we would go next, who my younger brother and I would live with, who would ultimately take care of us. I no longer looked at people with faith and trust but measured their kindness by imagined motives and conditions and judged people by appearances.

It wasn't just the ending of their marriage, because people divorce every day and can stay amicable for their children. It was what my parents became. What started as a joint effort; a team of four; a tribe who vacationed together, laughed together, went to church together, and did life together degenerated when the original two outgrew each other and no longer wanted to share their lives. My brain couldn't figure that out. Marriage was no longer until death do you part, and everything I had believed slipped away as water running out of a glass and escaping off the table.

Have you experienced that—you held something to be true and then one morning woke up and found everything changed? Before we can go any further, I need to ask you, seriously and with interest in your answer, Has that happened to you? Was there any specific time or event in your life when you began to question your identity and the nature of who God created you to be? Maybe it wasn't just one event but a series of events that made you question who you are.

There is typically one moment in time when the break occurs, leaving you lying in a heap on the floor with your whole world crashing in around you. But unlike having a bone fracture that needs time to heal, we get up from the floor and continue on with our lives, until before long we're used to the limp and the pain we feel as we take each step. We become numb to how the events in our life have knocked us off our original path and redefined our perception of true beauty. We're now traveling a new road, living a life of detours and disappointments and hungry for something we've forgotten we ever had—joy. All the while we are living this new life on a foundation of our pain, our past, and the lies we've been believing from the enemy. We're filled with the awareness of limitations, the fragmentation of broken promises, and the sensation of traveling in a desert with no hope for a promised land.

I traveled in this desert for 17 years. The day my foundation broke a fissure opened deep within me, cracking through the spiritual realm and breaking the mirror of how I knew God saw me. My body instantly went into "self-preservation" mode. If you look up "self-preservation" in the dictionary, you'll see that it's defined as the instinct to act in your own best interest to protect yourself and ensure survival.

What can I do to protect myself? I silently screamed. *How can I stop this pain and the feeling that I have no control?* When it's a matter of your physical survival, instantly your body reacts and you either run, jump, or move your arms to avoid injury. But when the pain and the perceived threat are in your heart, you don't realize that your mind begins to create another kind of defense mechanism. Before you know it, you revert to a pattern of behavior designed to ensure that you will never get hurt like that again.

My heart told me in a whisper: *Build a wall.* Being 11 years old, I didn't know what that meant. In my mind, I visualized the walls of sand I had built on the shores of Lake Michigan, camping with my family. I envisioned the sun on my face and the sand between my toes and felt safe. So I set out to look for driftwood in my life to construct my wall.

What I imagined became a symbol for how I would handle this and other, coming crises. I built a wall around me, and when I thought it was high enough I tried to pack sand into all the crevices. But my vulnerability kept spilling out. No matter how hard I tried to seal out the pain, guilt began to seep into all the openings, and an overpowering feeling of shame came over me. I was the reason they were getting a divorce. It was my fault. I was to blame. I was a mistake.

Soon everything gave way, and I stood there with my broken-down wall and wept inside. Clouds overtook the sun; it was now dark and lonely, and I could do only the one thing—the same thing I did every day before walking out the door to school: I grabbed my backpack. I stuffed inside the pile of sand from the broken-down wall. I packed in the guilt and shame and lies. I stuffed in all the dreams that were never going to come true, and I zipped the zipper shut. No one would hurt me again. I was okay. It was going to be okay. I was fine. And my journey began. It was as if I turned the page and started reading an alternate ending to a story that I had grown to love. The enemy of my soul had deviously whispered to my young heart, and I had believed. I was confident this was the only way I could live this life. And each heartbreak caused me to shift my weight, adjust my backpack, and continue to pick up more and more luggage. I just needed to keep moving. I just needed to keep pretending.

Fast forward, and I'm married, have two children fourteen months apart, and have been too long in the desert. I've absorbed every blow, every lie, every detour, and now my body is physically manifesting my pain. I developed shingles at 26 years old. After countless appointments and sitting with doctors answering a myriad of questions, the diagnosis came: bipolar disorder. The enemy had me exactly where he wanted me; isolated, alone, and wanting to end my life.

Aren't you curious? I mean, I was. How would my life be different if my foundation would have stayed built on the Lord? Who would I be today if I hadn't believed the lies from the enemy and drifted away from who God had designed me to be? My view of beauty would be different. I would be more courageous and loving and confident of my path. I would know true joy.

But the incredible thing—the thing that stops me in my tracks and makes me turn my face to the heavens and ask "Really, God?"—is His grace. He never stopped pursuing me, and He's never stopped pursuing you. He never stops calling our names in that desert we're plodding through. He never quits loving us even when we walk off the path. He calls us to return. He puts people in our lives to love us and help us and pray for us. He uses testimonies to change our perceptions and our thinking. He orchestrates opportunities to speak truth with love into our lives and asks us to allow Him to restore, reform, and renew us. He gives us chance after chance to believe the truth and to rebuke the enemy and his lies.

I'm here to tell you that there is hope! If you are experiencing depression or sadness or are just tired of traveling through detours and disappointments, don't let the enemy steal one more day. If you're curious and ready, then let's do this! Let's rebuild our foundations on God's Word, not the world. Let's leave behind the detours and disappointments and use the directions God gives us. Let's build our foundation on Him and find our joy again!

Diving Deeper

BREAKOUT

Please use the following pages to answer Chapter 1 questions, take notes, dig deeper, and journal on your journey toward finding joy again.

BREAKOUT QUESTIONS

Questions to think about, discuss, and answer:

1. What is YOUR definition of beauty?

2. How do you look at yourself?

3. Can you identify "the break" that may have happened in your life?

4. What have been your biggest disappointments?

5. Have you been on a detour? Explain.

6. Do you believe that God is actively pursuing you? What is He showing you right now?

7. Spend time in God's Word. Read Mark 5:1–20 and ask yourself this question: Why did Jesus go across the lake in the first place?

NOTES

DIVING DEEPER

Why did Jesus cross the lake in the first place? He crossed to help one man. A man who was possessed and was so out of control that those around him tried to chain him. But even chains couldn't hold him. When I think of this story, I put myself in this man's sandals. I was so lost, so out of my mind, that I didn't make good decisions; and so sad, so hopeless that I wanted to take my own life. And even while Jesus was on His way to help me, the enemy was trying to block Him from coming. He caused a storm, and the boat rocked and the wind blew. But God . . . ! Jesus knew what was happening and rebuked the wind and calmed the seas. He crossed the lake anyway. And He didn't come to save thousands; He came to save just me.

On top of all that, that one man Jesus saved began to tell the Decapolis how much Jesus had done for him; all the people were amazed . . . and many believed. You see, God sent Jesus into the world to save us! He is our lifeline, and if we follow Him He'll show us how to walk this earth and prepare for us our heavenly home. And He won't waste one ounce of our pain! Our testimony will change lives for His glory. Praise God!

If you believe this and choose to follow Him, no matter what the enemy does to you it will not stop Jesus from getting to you. He'll cross the lake just for you every time. Amen!

PRAYER

Father God, Lord Jesus, Holy Spirit,

First of all, thank You for crossing the lake for me. Thank You for loving me so much that You came to save me. I am grateful and praise You, Lord. I admit that I've been carrying around lies, Lord, lies that I've been believing about myself. Some days it feels like suitcase after suitcase of lies, and I am ready to lay it all down at the foot of the cross.

I surrender those parts of myself, Lord: the broken pieces of my life, the disappointments, the detours I've taken, the hurt, the past, the people who have hurt me, and I give it all to You. Rush in, Lord, and let me feel Your love in a real and tangible way. Break my chains of bondage and deliver me, Lord. I receive Your love, Your forgiveness, Your healing. Keep going before me, Lord, and preparing the way. I praise You and thank You and I ask these things in Jesus' name. Amen.

JOURNAL

CHAPTER 2

Rebuilding Our Foundation on the Word, Not the World

So how do we change direction and make our way out of the desert? How do we stop staring at orange cones all day long, traveling at only 45 miles per hour and never getting to our destination? Well, when we're traveling in this world, trying to get from Point A to Point B, we use our GPS. We plug in our coordinates, and they create a path, typically the most direct route to where we're going. So why are we wandering around spiritually lost? Because we're not using the GPS God gave us. We're not relying on His Word.

After that break happens and the enemy moves in, we've lost our footing. But wait—did he move in, or was he already there? I think I'm getting ahead of myself. Let's travel back to that 11-year old girl and her foundation. I was raised in the Nazarene church. We went to church twice on Sundays and on Wednesday nights, and I went to

Sunday school and church camp. I was very familiar with the gospel and knew my B-I-B-L-E. My foundation was built on these things:

1. I believed in God.
2. I knew Jesus was His Son. I believed that He stepped down from His throne, came to earth as a baby, lived among us as the Son of God, and died on a cross while we were still sinners. That He rose again and conquered death, as a consequence of which we have everlasting life.
3. I believed in the Holy Spirit, and the third member of the Godhead, the Trinity.
4. I believed in God's Word, the Bible, and that this is where we find our truth.
5. I believed that Jesus is coming again to take us home to heaven.

But what I didn't recognize at my young age was that the devil has come to steal, kill, and destroy and that he uses one particular tool to distract us from knowing who we are in Christ—that tool is lies. When we start to believe those lies, we step off the path and lose our footing. Did he move in after the break, or was it he who caused my parents' marriage to end? If he has come to steal, kill, and destroy, what is it that he is stealing, killing, and destroying? Is he stealing our joy, killing our marriages, destroying truth? Yes, he is!

We need to recognize that our foundation is one of the most important things we build. If we are standing on sand—lies from the enemy, past pain, or aspects of the world like money, fame, pride, or self-motivation—we will not weather the storms that come our way. As Jesus said in Matthew 7:24–27: "Therefore everyone who hears these words of mine and puts them into practice is like a wise man who built his house on the rock. The rain came down, the streams rose, and the winds blew and beat against that house; yet it did not fall, because it had its foundation on the rock. But everyone who hears these words of mine and does not put them into practice is like a foolish man who built his house on sand. The rain came down, the streams rose, and the winds blew and beat against that house, and it fell with a great crash."

To rebuild our foundation, we need to erect it with *ALL* of the truth. We need to believe not only in God; Jesus, His Son; the realities that Jesus died on the cross, rose again from the dead, and is coming again; the Holy Spirit; and God's Word, which is our truth . . . we need also to believe that the devil, our enemy, has come to steal, kill, and destroy. We need to believe that there is a spiritual battle going on and that his window of opportunity to kill, steal, and destroy is closing. His seemingly frenetic degree of activity is obvious as we look at this world and everything that is happening. We are seeing increased rates of suicide, mass shootings, sex-trafficking, legalized partial-birth abortion, extreme poverty, war and terrorism, drug abuse, disease, racism, murder, and political unrest. We need to wake up and realize that we are battling for our very lives and that there has never been more urgency than right now.

In an article written by Kenneth Copeland titled "Why Is It So Important to Meditate on God's WORD?" Copeland writes:

> So many born-again believers miss out on the world-overcoming victory that's theirs in Christ Jesus. They keep finding themselves "under" the circumstances instead of "on top," and they can't figure out why. They've never understood a foundational truth about living the successful Christian life. They've never understood why it is so important to meditate on, or ponder and contemplate, the WORD of God.

Proverbs 4:20–22 says, "My son, pay attention to what I say; turn your ear to my words. Do not let them out of your sight, keep them within your heart; for they are life to those who find them and health to one's whole body."

Notice that, according to those verses, when you "attend" to God's words, they become "sayings." The Scriptures start talking to you. The Holy Spirit speaks them to you on the inside so you can not only see but also hear the thoughts of God. If you'll make the decision to internalize those thoughts by repeating them on purpose over and over again, eventually you'll catch yourself saying them without having to decide to do so. When that happens, your thinking in that area has been converted. God's thoughts have become your own.

When we are not "attending" to God's Word but wandering around a desert, unsure of where to go, Satan will use every trick in his arsenal to persuade and distract us so that we will turn our eyes . . . and our feet will follow. He is the author of lies and has watched our families for generations, knowing what we struggle with and what lies we need to hear. That is the truth. He'll seduce us with liquor and medications and numb our core so that we cannot discern the Holy Spirit. He'll whisper our name and fill us with pride until we feel bulletproof and then sit back and watch the crash. His only goal is to kill, steal, and destroy and take with him as many as he can before Jesus comes again.

Why do so many born-again believers find themselves "under," instead of "on top of," their circumstances, as Kenneth Copeland noted? Because we are not meditating on the truth of God's Word. We've slipped into a state of complacency, feeding on the spoon-fed lies the enemy offers us each day. My friends, why would we do this when we can have fresh bread and wine with our Lord Jesus Christ? Why would we believe that we are hopeless, damaged goods, with no future and no purpose, when we can claim and declare that we are sons and daughters of the Most High King? We are loved. We are cherished. Our sins were paid for on the cross. And He is coming again to bring us home. Amen.

Whatever you have been claiming as your truth, ask the Lord today to reveal His truth to you. Spend time in His Word. Ask God to show you the changes He wants you to make in your daily life so He can be in relationship with you. Then keep taking one step at a time forward, out of the desert and into the promised land.

We don't have to be "under" the circumstances of this fallen world. There will be trouble, we will have struggles, and we will experience the hardships of being human and all that this entails. But no weapon formed against us shall prosper! He who is in us is GREATER—infinitely so—than he who is in the world, and we need to start believing that and declaring this truth over our lives. When we meditate on God's Word and His truth, the lies become just that, and we can disregard anything the enemy whispers in our ear.

After the break happened when my parents told me they were getting a divorce, it was not only my world that broke apart but the mirror I looked into to see how God looked at me. My perception changed. The broken mirror was replaced with a different one from the enemy. And that mirror has rejected me countless times, because it distorted the way I saw myself. That mirror didn't look back at me with nonjudgmental eyes and unconditional love. When I looked into that mirror, I saw all of my flaws, failures, and disappointments and could hardly fathom that God could love me.

The first step in renewing our minds is to start seeing ourselves as God sees us. We need to recognize that we've made mistakes and sinned but that Jesus has forgiven us and removed our transgressions as far as the east is from the west. We need to stand on His truth and believe His Word: "But he said to me, 'My grace is sufficient for you, for my power is made perfect in weakness.' Therefore I will boast all the more gladly of my weaknesses, so that Christ's power may rest on me. That is why, for Christ's sake, I delight in weaknesses, in insults, in hardships, in persecutions, in difficulties. For when I am weak, then I am strong" (2 Corinthians 12:9–10).

After reading all of this, maybe you're asking yourself *What is my current foundation?* Well, here are some factors to consider: Do you look for approval from others? Do you assess your value according to how well you do your job or from the perspective of your spouse or children or friends? Or maybe you don't even look for approval but compare your life unfavorably to other people's.

When we seek affirmation from the people around us, we're no longer looking in the mirror but seeing ourselves through the eyes of someone else. This is fine when they look at us with love, but what happens when their opinion of us changes—or even when we just think or worry that it has? What happens when they're in a bad mood or going through a challenging season or are simply distracted and don't have a positive word for us? Does our value change? No. Did we change? Not necessarily.

For many years I hid behind a mask, wearing an "I'm Fine" t-shirt and carrying around all of my luggage—, trying to make everyone believe that I *was* fine. I wanted to see myself through their eyes. I wanted to believe that I was exactly the who I was showing them. But the truth was that I felt like damaged goods. I felt like I needed to pretend to be someone else, because no one could possibly love me for who I was. But, of course, that was a lie. Jesus loves me and died on a cross to save me, just as He loves you and died for you.

What I had to learn is that the enemy wants to isolate us and make us feel as though we're all alone. He wants our perceptions to be skewed in such a way that we look at others and think, *Look, they have it all together. Look, they never fight. Look how good their kids are. Look how thin she is. Look at how good his job is. You'll never measure up to them. Look, look, look . . .*

The problem is that when you look to others for affirmation or comparison, you never know which of you— if not both—is wearing that "I'm fine" shirt. Everyone has problems, my friends. Everyone has difficulties. But in those difficult times, instead of declaring "I'm fine," we need to share with someone how we are really doing and ask for prayer. We all have struggles and issues and heartaches; I can tell you that I traveled for years believing I was the only one who did. But when we shine light into the dark areas of our life, we permit God to do His work in us and heal us from our brokenness. And when we tear down our walls and stop pretending, we can see that other people struggle too, and we together become more like the true body of Christ. A family. Lifting each other up and walking alongside each other, in good times and in bad. To have true joy, we need to be original—our own original, the way God designed us to be. And when His opinion of us means more to us than anyone else's and we can see ourselves clearly, not in our own distorted mirror or through someone else's eyes, we are traveling down a path of true freedom. We need to stay rooted in His love, because God's opinion of us will never change.

Whatever your current foundation, it's never too late! It's time to build our lives on the rock. We know that the rain will come and the streams will rise and the winds will blow. We now know whom to believe in and that we *are* in a spiritual battle. But we also know that "no weapon forged against [us] will prevail" (Isaiah 54:17). To fight in this battle, we need to hold fast to our foundation and get ready. And to do that we must put on the full armor of God. Are you ready?

Diving Deeper

BREAKOUT

Please use the following pages to answer Chapter 2 questions, take notes, dig deeper, and journal on your journey toward finding joy again.

BREAKOUT QUESTIONS

Please use the space below to write your answers, dig deeper, and journal on your journey toward finding joy again.

Questions to think about, discuss, and answer:

1. Of, or on, what is your current foundation laid?

2. Do you look for affirmation from others?

3. What do you see when you look in the mirror?

4. Have you ever put on an "I'm fine" shirt? Are you wearing one right now?

5. Do you believe that you are in a spiritual battle?

6. Spend time in God's Word. Read Matthew 7:24–27 and be reminded of the kind of foundation you need to have.

NOTES

DIVING DEEPER

So why are we struggling to find our joy? We're realizing that our foundation has been built on the world, not the WORD. When we look to others for our affirmation, look in the mirror for approval, or hope in anything but the Lord, our foundation will crumble and we will lose our joy. I know this, because there was a time when I stood before the mirror in the bathroom, with pills in the palm of my hand, and had no hope. I had hoped in myself but failed daily because I could not overcome my mental illness. I had hoped in my husband, but he wasn't happy and couldn't lift me from my own sorrow. I had hoped in my children, but as much as they loved me they couldn't help me emotionally. I had hoped in the doctors, but all they could do was prescribe the very pills I held in my hand. There was only one person I had not hoped in, and that was Jesus. I had asked Him time and again to heal me and take this illness from me, but I believed He didn't care. I believed this request was too big for Him. I believed He had forgotten me. But these were all lies from the enemy. When our foundation is not built on the WORD, we will forget God's promises and lose sight of who we really are: sons and daughters of the Most High King. Today we are taking back what the enemy has stolen from us. We are rebuilding our foundation on God's WORD and renewing our minds. If you're ready, say this prayer with me:

PRAYER

Father God, Lord Jesus, Holy Spirit,

I know I'm a sinner, and I ask for Your forgiveness. I believe Jesus Christ is Your Son. I believe that He died for my sins and that You raised Him to life. I believe in the Holy Spirit and that He lives inside me. I believe in Your Word and that I need to renew my mind with it every day so that it is my solid foundation. I want to trust You as my Savior and follow You every day from this day forward. Guide my life and help me to do Your will. I pray this in the glorious name of Jesus. Amen.

JOURNAL

CHAPTER 3

Putting on the Full Armor of God, Because It's a Battle

I remember when I was a little girl, standing up in church reciting the Apostles' Creed. We would stand as a congregation, our hearts and voices unified, declaring the truth that we believed. I would say each word with confidence:

I believe in God,
The Father Almighty,
creator of heaven and earth.
I believe in Jesus Christ, his only Son, our Lord,
who was conceived by the Holy Spirit,
born of the Virgin Mary,
suffered under Pontius Pilate,
was crucified, died, and was buried;
he descended to the dead.
On the third day he rose again;

he ascended into heaven,
is seated at the right hand of the Father,
and will come again to judge the living and the dead.

I believe in the Holy Spirit,
the holy Christian church,
the communion of saints,
the forgiveness of sins,
the resurrection of the body,
and the life everlasting.
Amen.

But as I look back now, I so wish we had just as regularly declared some other truths, truths that I've discovered as I've lived in this world: like the fact that there is an enemy who has come to steal, kill, and destroy. The Bible tells us that he prowls around like a roaring lion, waiting for someone to devour, but this rarely gets mentioned from many pulpits, and the battle we experience rages on without a name or an understanding.

I'm here to tell you that the battle is real! We face an enemy we cannot see and fight a battle, not with physical weapons but with spiritual ones. But what happens when we don't even realize we're in this battle? We move through our lives day in and day out struggling—listening to lie after lie, believing that we are anything but the sons and daughters of the God who created us for a plan and a purpose. We wake up one day to find that our joy has been stolen, our families are divided, our children are deprived of their identity, and our health is hanging in the balance. It's as though we were struck in the night, we're injured and bleeding, and our adversary has walked off with all the spoils.

So now that we're aware that we're in this battle for our very lives, how do we fight? What weapons do we use to win? The Bible is very clear when we go there for the answer:

"Finally, be strong in the Lord and in his mighty power. Put on the full armor of God, so that you can take your stand against the devil's schemes. For our struggle is not against flesh and blood, but against the rulers, against the authorities, against the powers of this dark world and against the spiritual forces of evil in the heavenly realms. Therefore put on the full armor of God, so that when the day of evil comes, you may be able to stand your ground, and after you have done everything, to stand. Stand firm then, with the belt of truth buckled around your waist, with the breastplate of righteousness in place, and with your feet fitted with the readiness that comes from the gospel of peace. In addition to all this, take up the shield of faith, with which you can extinguish all the flaming arrows of the evil one. Take the helmet of salvation and the sword of the Spirit, which is the Word of God. And pray in the Spirit on all occasions with all kinds of prayers and requests. With this in mind, be alert and always keep on praying for all the Lord's people" (Ephesians 6:10–18).

I know what you're thinking: "the armor of God, I've heard of that." Well, I had too. But the more I understood about spiritual battles and what they felt like, the more I started to understand the importance of that armor and how I needed to do more than just know about it . . . I needed to put it on, every day! So, let's look at each piece and understand its importance and how they all work together.

The Belt of Truth

"Stand firm then, with the belt of truth buckled around your waist," Paul says. Why is the belt of truth so important? It holds all of the other pieces of armor in place. We need to understand scriptural truth, as opposed to the lies of the enemy. We need to stand on the only firm foundation—on truth based on the Word of God. To acknowledge that we are loved. That we are forgiven. That we have hope. That Jesus died for our sins and is coming again to take us home.

The Breastplate of Righteousness

" . . . with the breastplate of righteousness in place." When we put on the breastplate of righteousness, it covers our heart and guards it, along with all our other vital organs. It also protects us against all of Satan's accusations. The Bible says, "Above all else, guard your heart, for everything you do flows from it" (Proverbs 4:23).

The breastplate is not comprised of our righteousness, because the Bible is clear that none of us is righteous in ourselves (Romans 3:10). It is made up of Christ's righteousness, which He gives us freely when we accept Him as our Savior.

Shoes of the Gospel

I know that we as women can resonate with this one: shoes! In my case, I have two-hour shoes, six-hour shoes, and eight-hour shoes. And I have definitely worn them all at the wrong times. Paul says here, " . . . and with your feet fitted with the readiness that comes from the gospel of peace." We don't have to dress for success, but we do have to dress for marching, and I love this permission. We need to put on these gospel shoes that will allow us to march wherever the Lord leads.

The Shield of Faith

Paul writes, "In addition to all this, take up the shield of faith, with which you can extinguish all the flaming arrows of the evil one." Faith. The apostle states in Romans 12:3 that God gifts each of us a measure of faith. To repeat, in case you've missed it, faith is a gift. We then need to grow our faith by fellowshipping with Lord and spending time in His Word until our measure grows and develops. We can then pick up this shield and block the devil's fiery darts of doubt, his tempting list of lies, and live a victorious life, confident of who we are and whose we are.

The Helmet of Salvation

"Take the helmet of salvation." When we put on the helmet, it protects our head, perhaps the most vital part of our body. Our brain is the organ with which we think and process and dream. We need to protect our thoughts and not allow the enemy to penetrate our minds. We need to be confident of our truth and certain that our foundation is rooted and based on the Word of God.

The Sword of the Spirit

" . . . and the sword of the Spirit, which is the word of God." While all the other armor of God is defensive in nature, the sword of the Spirit is the weapon used for offense. Hebrews 4:12 describes God's Word as "alive and active. Sharper than any double-edged sword." It was Jesus himself who showed us how to pick up this sword and fight against the enemy. While He was tempted for forty days and nights in the desert, he fought the enemy by using this very sword: "It is written . . . " (e.g., Matthew 4:4). God's truth is powerful and will not only protect us from our enemy, the devil, but will help us fight when he tempts us.

Paul closes by saying "And pray in the Spirit on all occasions with all kinds of prayers and requests. With this in mind, be alert and always keep on praying for all the Lord's people" (Ephesians 6:18). It's not enough to just put on the full armor of God every day; we need to cover it all with prayer. This can be prayers that we say over ourselves or when we join our brothers and sisters in Christ and go to war with them.

We've looked at each piece of the armor and have a better understanding of why each one is necessary and how it allows us to be ready for combat. We understand the importance of prayer and how we need it in our arsenal. But what about the Bible? We established in chapter 2 that the Bible is like our GPS while we're living in this world. Are you in God's Word each day and building and internalizing your cache of truth?

I know that the Bible can be challenging to read. We typically start out really strong in Genesis, make our way through Exodus, get into Leviticus, . . . and find ourselves lost in Numbers. But what we have to remember is that the writers of each book were writing to the people of their time. They were using imagery and language those people would understand. That is why it's important to not just read God's Word but to study it and meditate on it. We need to dig in, google passages, and explore Bible commentaries.

For example, when looking at Ephesians 6:12, some translations refer to "struggle": "For our struggle is not against flesh and blood, . . . " But if you look at the King James Version, the word "wrestle" is used: "For we *wrestle* not against flesh and blood . . ." (emphasis added). This one word changes everything. Paul was writing this to the readers of his time. To set the stage for this imagery, Perry Stone, author of *There's a Crack in Your Armor*, writes:

> There were many different games in which men competed during the Greek Olympics or during the times of various festivals. However, wrestling is different because of three things.
>
> 1. You must always face your opponent and never turn your back, as if you turn, you will be slammed to the ground and penned in a dangerous position.
> 2. You must always watch and make eye contact with your opponent, otherwise a sudden move will be made that will catch you off guard, giving the advantage to your opponent.
> 3. The third aspect is that wrestling is the only sport in which you will never lose physical contact with your opponent. Thus, wrestling is a face-to-face, eye-to-eye, hand-to-hand, and body-to-body contact sport. In the believer's case, it is not a sport but a matter of life and death.

Perry Stone points out to the reader why Paul from his context may have used the equivalent of the English word "wrestle." The people of that time would have witnessed the sport, watching the two men face off, always keeping their eyes on each other, engaged in hand-to-hand combat. When we see that we are in a life-and-death wrestling match with the enemy, it puts things into perspective. We are battling for our very lives. We need to be ready for combat. We need to put on the full armor of God, keep our eyes on the enemy, carry our sword (the Word of God), and know which verses to cite when we cry out "IT IS WRITTEN . . . !"

The Bible is our truth. But just because it can be challenging at times to understand, it's necessary, and certainly not impossible to do so, as the devil would like you to believe. Satan knows that you will find everything you need in God's Word to live this life, and he also knows that he will easily be defeated if we understand his strategies and fight our battle using God's truth.

Let's take a moment to understand why. What are the devil's goals? His greatest desire is to distract us, to push us out of fellowship with God. He will lie to us, isolate us, and break us until we feel alone, lost, and ready to believe every lie he is whispering to us. When we are isolated and alone, flailing around like a rag doll through the storms of this life, without our joy we may continue down this path until we are so sad, so lost, so confused . . . that we just want to end it all. I know—I have been there. And that's exactly where he wants us: isolated and alone, wanting to end our life.

In Priscilla Shirer's amazing book *The Armor of God*, she points out ten strategies that the enemy uses to attack, specifically, women. Take a look below and see whether you can recognize some of the ways in which the enemy has been attacking you . . .

Strategy #1 – Against Your Passion
He seeks to dim your whole desire for prayer, dull your interest in spiritual things, and downplay the potency of your most strategic weapons (Ephesians 6:10–20).

Strategy #2 – Against Your Focus
He disguises himself and manipulates your perspective so you end up focusing on the wrong culprit, directing your weapons at the wrong enemy (2 Corinthians 11:14).

Strategy #3 – Against Your Identity
He magnifies your insecurities, leading you to doubt what God says about you and to disregard what He has given you (Ephesians 1:17–19).

Strategy #4 – Against Your Family
He wants to disintegrate your family, dividing your home and rendering it chaotic, restless, and unfruitful (Genesis 3:1–7).

Strategy #5 – Against Your Confidence

He constantly reminds you of your past mistakes and bad choices, hoping to convince you that you're under God's judgement rather than under the blood (Revelation 12:10).

Strategy #6 – Against Your Calling

He amplifies fear, worry, and anxiety until they're the loudest voices in your head, causing you to deem the adventure of following God too risky to attempt (Joshua 14:8).

Strategy #7 – Against Your Purity

He tries to tempt you toward certain sins, convincing you that you can tolerate them without risking consequence, knowing that they'll only wedge distance between yourself and God (Isaiah 59:1–2).

Strategy #8 – Against Your Rest and Contentment

He hopes to overload your life and schedule, pressuring you to constantly push beyond your limits, never feeling permission to say no (Deuteronomy 5:15).

Strategy #9 – Against Your Heart

He uses every opportunity to keep old wounds fresh in your mind, knowing that anger and hurt and bitterness and unforgiveness will continue to roll the damage forward (Hebrews 12:15).

Strategy #10 – Against Your Relationships
He creates disruption and disunity within your circle of friends and within the shared community of the body of Christ (1 Timothy 2:8).

If you're like me, you can read each one of those strategies and know that you've been at war with the enemy. While he is not original, he is definitely cunning and consistent and has his own minions that can do his dirty work. And it's not just a battle that *we* are in; we need to put on the full armor of God to fight for our families, our loved ones, our neighbors, and even those we don't yet know. But remember: do not fear and do not be discouraged. "'No weapon that is forged against you will prevail, and you will refute every tongue that accuses you. This is the heritage of the servants of the LORD, and this is their vindication from me,' declares the LORD" (Isaiah 54:17).

As we continue our journey toward finding our joy again, the next stop is understanding the lies we've been believing and replacing those lies with God's truth. Let's keep moving forward, out of the desert and into the promised land . . .

Diving Deeper

BREAKOUT

Please use the following pages to answer Chapter 3 questions, take notes, dig deeper, and journal on your journey toward finding joy again.

BREAKOUT QUESTIONS

Please use the space below to write your answers, dig deeper, and journal on your journey toward finding joy again.

Questions to think about, discuss, and answer:

1. Do you now see that you are in a spiritual battle?

2. What strategies has the enemy been using against you?

3. Do you struggle with reading God's Word?

4. Think of some ways you can dig deeper into God's truth each day.
    a. Who can hold me accountable?
    b. Can I join a Bible study group?

5. Are you ready to put on the full armor of God and fight?

NOTES

DIVING DEEPER

Sometimes it can appear overwhelming to open our eyes and see another world. Yesterday it was just us, trying to live our lives, and today we realize that we are fighting an invisible war and told to put on the full armor of God. But can you see that He is leading us out of Egypt and away from our slavery? He is even orchestrating our way out of the desert, and now we're standing at the edge of Jordan, looking at the life that could be ours . . . We could stay in the desert, continuing to believe the lies and not living to our full potential in Christ. Or we could keep moving forward, into all the promises God has in store for us and into the kind of joy we can have only with Him. We have a choice. What will you choose?

PRAYER

Father God, Lord Jesus, Holy Spirit,

Thank you for opening my eyes. Thank you for allowing me to see this battle and for giving me the tools with which to fight. Help me to put on the full armor of God every day and to bathe all of the components in prayer. I lift up myself, my family, my neighbors, and those I do not know and pray for Your strength and Your truth. Thank You that You have already won this war! Thank You that You died on the cross to save me from my sins and that You conquered death. I love You. I praise You. I ask all of these things in your precious name. Amen.

JOURNAL

CHAPTER 4

Replacing the Lies with the Truth

When Moses and the Israelites reached the promised land, God had them send men into the land to report back about the people who lived there and what the land was like and to bring back a sampling of the fruits that grew there. They were gone for forty days, and when they returned they gave their account: "We went into the land to which you sent us, and it does flow with milk and honey! Here is its fruit. But the people who live there are powerful, and the cities are fortified and very large" (Numbers 13:27–28).

All the men but one said that they should not enter the land, that the people were bigger and stronger than they were, and that they would surely die there. All the people of the community began to cry out and lament, "If only we had died in Egypt! Or in this wilderness!"

What do you do when you stand at the edge of the promised land that the Lord is giving you? Do you doubt His promises and think of a million reasons you shouldn't enter? Or do you step in with faith and anticipation of all the things the Lord will do? I know this next step is not easy. It's not easy looking back, thinking about the lies we've believed. It's not easy digging in and doing the hard work or replacing those lies with God's truth. But we're not looking for temporary joy. We are renewing our minds so we can have an *abundance* of joy. We're renewing our minds so we can know without a doubt who we are in Christ.

I know all too well what it is to stand at this edge and look into the promised land. If you know my story, you know that I struggled with bipolar disorder and all of the consequences of the illness for 17 years. I divorced my husband, went through bankruptcy, struggled as a single mother, got remarried, and discovered that all of the baggage I was carrying around now affected my second marriage. I became so bitter and filled with resentment that it spilled over into every aspect of my life, and I no longer recognized the woman standing in front of the mirror. That distorted mirror that I ran to for affirmation once again labeled me unfit, unqualified, unloved, and now stuck in a second marriage where I would never measure up.

But God . . . ! Once again, He reached out to me through a friend who prayed for me and offered me an opportunity to engage in a day of prayer. While I had no idea what that even meant, I was desperate for change and thirsty from the years spent walking endlessly in the barren desert.

So, on March 22, 2013, I arrived at 10:00 a.m. for the day of prayer and didn't leave that night until after 8:00 p.m. It had taken all day, walking through each moment of my life; praying over every sin, every decision, every instance in which I had walked away from God. When I arrived, it looked as though I had been traveling on a yearlong trip, with all my suitcases and baggage. But when I left—I walked out carrying only my purse. I had laid down all the baggage at the foot of the cross and relinquished all the bitterness, resentment, fear, shame, guilt, and confusion. But more than that, Jesus not only healed me from a lifetime of wrong choices and painful misconceptions but of the mental illness that was supposed to stay with me for the rest of my life. My chains were broken, and I was free to live the life that God had intended for me all along!

When I looked back at the day of healing and everything I had been carrying around in those suitcases, it occurred to me that even though I left those suitcases at the foot of the cross, I had to understand what I had believed to be true and how it had affected me. I had to unpack the lies so I could replace those lies with truth.

The truth is that the enemy is a liar. The truth is that the enemy has come to steal, kill, and destroy, that he is prowling around like a roaring lion looking for someone to devour. The truth is that he is constantly whispering lies to us, and when we start to believe them it will affect our clarity of mind, our relationships, our jobs, and our ability to trust God. The truth is that it's never too late to rebuke the cold whisper in your ear, . . . and that's exactly what I did.

Once my foundation was established and rebuilt, I needed to speak truth into all the areas of my life where I had been broken, so I would never pick up those suitcases again. I needed to start with the lie that had done the most damage, so I started at the beginning, 43 years earlier, on that warm day of June. It wasn't by accident that I had entered this world. Even though my parents were young and without a plan, God had a plan, and it included me. I would no longer believe that I was anything but chosen and loved by God. I would believe that I was His beloved.

So let's talk about some of the lies we believe. Review the list below and see whether these are some of the things that cross your mind on a daily basis:

I am unloved.
I am unworthy.
I am a failure.
I am fearful.
I am weak.
I am depressed.
I can't reach God.

Have these words played over in your mind? Are these statements that ring regularly in your ears? My friends, these are lies! This kind of self-talk is what the enemy uses to decimate our foundation and destroy who we are in Christ. We need to reprogram ourselves and renew our minds; instead of listening to the enemy, we need to hear what Jesus says about us. We need to replace those lies with the Word of God. Right now, we are going to go through each lie, cross it out, and read what God's Word has to say:

Cross out "I am unloved" and read John 15:9–11:
"As the Father has loved me, so have I loved you. Now remain in my love. If you keep my commands, you will remain in my love, just as I have kept my Father's commands and remain in his love. I have told you this so that *my joy may be in you and that your joy may be complete"* (emphasis added).

I went after many things in this life that I thought would bring me joy. A nice house didn't do it, money didn't do it, my husband's love didn't do it, nor did my friends. Only Jesus can give us true joy. Being in fellowship with Him and knowing without a doubt that He loves us will bring us the kind of joy we need while living in this world. And the enemy knows that if he can distract us from *remaining* in His love, our foundation will crumble. You are loved! Believe that today.

Cross Out "I am unworthy" and read 1 Corinthians 6:19–20:
"Do you not know that your bodies are temples of the Holy Spirit, who is in you, whom you have received from God? You are not your own; you were bought at a price. Therefore honor God with your bodies."

How can we be unworthy if we were bought at a price? Jesus died for us! We are oh, so special and loved. We *are* worthy, not because of who we are but because of who loves us! That's what we have to remember, and that's what we have to remind the enemy when he whispers in our ear.

Cross out "I am a failure" and read Romans 8:37–39:
"No, in all these things we are more than conquerors through him who loved us. For I am convinced that neither death nor life, neither angels nor demons, neither the present nor the future, nor any powers, neither height nor depth, nor anything else in all creation, will be able to separate us from the love of God that is in Christ Jesus our Lord."

My friends, nothing we do will make us a failure in God's eyes. And He is the One we should be looking to. We will never be able to make everyone else happy. We as humans are all broken people living in a sin-filled world. And if we are rating our success based on the world's opinion of us instead of on God's, we will never measure up.

Cross out "I am fearful" and read 1 John 4:18:
"There is no fear in love. But perfect love drives out fear, because fear has to do with punishment. The one who fears is not made perfect in love."

God *is* love! It's His very identity. And if God is love, and there is no fear in love, then we should have no fear. Fear comes from the enemy. When we're afraid, we can become paralyzed and unable to do all the things God is calling us to do. And the enemy knows this. Be reminded by meditating on His Word of how much God loves us and that there is no fear in love. The number of times love is mentioned in the Bible depends on the translation. In the NIV the word *love* is mentioned 551 times—319 times in the Old Testament and 232 times in the New Testament. That's 551 reminders that perfect love drives out fear.

Cross out "I am weak" and read Acts 1:8:
"But you will receive power when the Holy Spirit comes on you; and you will be my witnesses in Jerusalem, and in all Judea and Samaria, and to the ends of the earth."

There are other verses in the Bible that talk about being strong in Christ, so why this one? Because when the Holy Spirit transforms us, we are transformed in the likeness of Jesus—and Jesus is *not* weak! We need to remember that we are not weak, either; we are strong in Christ—a reality the enemy does not want us to recognize or believe. If you believe the truth that you're strong, he cannot use you, manipulate you, or steal your joy. Amen!

Cross out "I am depressed" and read Romans 15:13:
"May the God of hope fill you will all joy and peace as you trust in him, so that you may overflow with hope by the power of the Holy Spirit."

These very words tell us that God is a God of hope, joy, and peace. I know this to be a fact: depression comes from the enemy. I spent years trapped in sadness, focusing on everything negative that was happening to me and missing out on the abundant life God had for me. When we are depressed, swimming in sadness, we are exactly where the enemy wants us: isolated, alone, gasping for breath, and sometimes even wanting to end it all. This is the enemy's true intention for us: to steal not only our joy but our very lives.

If you are depressed, contemplating desperate thoughts, reach out to someone right now. Allow God's light, truth, and love to penetrate that sadness and help you break those chains. God is a God of joy, and He wants you to have that joy today.

Cross out "I can't reach God" and read 1 John 5:14–15:
"This is the confidence we have in approaching God: that if we ask anything according to his will, he hears us. And if we know that he hears us—whatever we ask—we know that we have what we asked of him."

I heard in my head too many times declarations like God doesn't love you, He can't heal you, He doesn't care. But those are all lies. He does love us—infinitely so—and we have full access to His throne because of Jesus. When Jesus died, the curtain that separated the Most Holy Place was torn in two, from top to bottom, giving us access to God our Father. Oswald Chambers said it well when he talked about what Jesus did on the cross:

> It was the supreme triumph, and it shook the very foundations of hell. There is nothing in time or eternity more absolutely certain and irrefutable than what Jesus accomplished on the cross. He made it possible for the entire human race to be brought back into a right-standing relationship with God. He made redemption the foundation of human life; that is, He made a way for every person to have fellowship with God.

So, when you hear "I can't reach God" and all the other lies the enemy will try to tell you, know they are exactly that: lies. Remember, our truth comes from the Word, not the world. Replace each lie you have been believing and stand on your new foundation with confidence, remembering who you are in Christ. And what does Jesus say about the truth? "The truth will set you free" (John 8:32).

What do you do when you stand at the edge of the promised land the Lord is giving you? Do you doubt His promises and think of a million reasons you shouldn't enter? Or do you step forward with faith, hope, and anticipation of all the things the Lord will do? I want to encourage you that it's time to cross over. It's time for us to leave the desert, where we've traveled for so long, lay our suitcases down at the foot of the cross, and make our way triumphantly into the promised land. Because in order for us to keep our joy while we live in this world, we need to remember that "faith is confidence in what we hope for and assurance about what we do not see" (Hebrews 11:1).

Diving Deeper

BREAKOUT

Please use the following pages to answer Chapter 4 questions, take notes, dig deeper, and journal on your journey toward finding joy again.

BREAKOUT QUESTIONS

Please use the space below to write your answers, dig deeper, and journal on your journey toward finding joy again.

Questions to think about, discuss, and answer:

1. Make a list of the lies you have been believing.

2. Replace each lie with God's truth. If you can't find the biblical reference, use Google. Type in "Bible verse that talks about _____" and then type in the lie.

3. Write out your new truth on an index card and place the cards strategically throughout your home, in places where you will be reminded.

4. Are you ready to lay your baggage down at the foot of the cross?

5. Are you ready to step into your promised land? What are your fears?

NOTES

DIVING DEEPER

It's sometimes challenging to know what to do when you keep hearing the lies. But each time the lie comes back up, you need to rebuke the enemy and say no. Say it out loud and with authority: "No, I'm not going to believe that. My God says this about me: _____. And I'm going to believe Him. Now GO in Jesus' name!" So this week when you are discerning your thoughts, ask yourself these questions: Did what I just heard edify me, assure me, stretch me, or feed me? Because that's what happens when the Father speaks to us. Even when He rebukes us, He does it in a loving way. And if the answer is no, then rebuke the enemy and command him to leave in Jesus' name. He has to flee, my friends. He will not stand in a roomful of light.

If you're struggling, here are some examples of what you can do to quiet your mind and take action:

- Put on the full armor of God. It's never too late.
- Start saying the name of Jesus out loud.
- Phone a friend for prayer.
- Turn on some Christian music and start praising Jesus.
- Change your location.
- Take a shower.
- Take a walk.

PRAYER

Father God, Lord Jesus, Holy Spirit,

Thank You for Your truth! Thank You that You gave me everything I would need in Your Word. Help me, Lord, to fight. Speak to my heart, heal my wounds, and tell me exactly what I need to hear and believe in order to replace the lies I have been believing from the enemy. I'm ready to cross over. I'm ready to experience the life that You have planned for me. I want the kind of joy that only You can give. I love You. I praise You. Please continue to go before me and prepare the way. I ask all of these things in the mighty name of Jesus. Amen.

JOURNAL

CHAPTER 5

Faith and Hope Bring Joy

If you would've asked me ten years ago, "What does faith mean to me?" my answer would've been vague. " . . . You know, you need to believe in God. Faith is believing without seeing." But while that is partly true, my journey toward discovering who I am in Christ has opened countless doors of "truth" that have revealed that faith is much more than that.

On the other hand, I felt all along that I understood the meaning of hope. Hope is commonly used as synonymous with a wish—its potency dependent upon the person doing the hoping and the relative importance of the wish to that person. I had hoped for years. My desire for healing and a normal way of life was so tangible that if this could have been captured as an exercise on a fit-bit, I would've burned real calories. But what I didn't know is that "Bible," or biblical, hope is different. Bible hope is the confident expectation of what God has promised, and its strength is not in our desire but in God's faithfulness.

That is where I struggled. I was hoping in my own strength. I was seeing life with my physical eyes, feeling all of its disappointments and traveling through detour after detour. When I couldn't tangibly feel change, I lost my hope. The Bible tells us that the righteous who have this trustful hope in God have a generalized confidence in God's protection and help (Jeremiah 29:11) and are free from fear and anxiety (Psalm 46:2–3). My life was filled with anxiety, and I had no confidence that the Lord cared for me and wanted to help me. I traveled day in and day out feeling alone and unloved and believing every lie from the enemy.

Feelings. That was my other problem; faith and feelings are two different things. I rode a rollercoaster of feelings for years. My diagnosis of bipolar disorder came with an internal operating manual of emotional triggers and frenzied feelings. In this life we are going to "feel" all kinds of things, and a lot of those feelings are associated with what's going on around us. But believe it or not, just because we feel something doesn't mean it's the appropriate emotion. How we react emotionally goes back to our foundation. If we are reacting based on our past—our hurts, our trials, our feelings—our reaction will be consistent not with God's Word but with our own perceived reality.

So how do we navigate faith and hope? What I'm learning is that we have to look to God's Word every time we have a question like this in life. And then we need to dig in. Digging in could mean meditating on God's Word, conducting a Bible study, reading Bible commentaries, or working under a mentor. And maybe all of the above. In my case, God connected me with an amazing mentor who gave me the material to start understanding the core principles of the Bible and how they worked together. For the first time in my life, the pieces started coming together, and my "truth" started to become as real and tangible as a physical puzzle coming together piece by piece into a recognizable entity. I laid those pieces out on the table, and the picture that formed was incredible.

One of the books I was given to read was *Bible Faith* by Kenneth Hagin. I wasn't familiar with Mr. Hagin, but after reading the back jacket of his book I learned that "he ministered for almost 70 years after God miraculously healed him of a deformed heart and an incurable blood disease at the age of 17. Even though Rev. Hagin went home to be with the Lord in 2003, the ministry he founded continues to bless multitudes around the globe." I was positive this man had to know something about faith.

I discovered that this book was considered college material and wasn't a quick read. But I wasn't looking for a quick fix. I needed my foundation to include faith and hope—components I had lacked for years. So I read each word out loud, underlining and highlighting as I went along. I allowed the Holy Spirit to renew my mind and carved out time each week to read a chapter and answer the study questions. I met with my mentor to go over what I had learned and was able to ask her questions and pray over my progress. This took *time*. And I'm *still* learning, . . . as I will be until my very last day.

I think that sometimes we're looking for microwave answers. It doesn't help that we live in a microwave society; it isn't only about fast food being delivered, hot and ready to our door but also about turbo tax, instant whitening toothpaste, stores open twenty-four hours, and a computer in the palm of our hand that can transport us across the globe with one click and answer virtually any factual question without pause. With this mindset, how do we make room for God and His truth? A God who was quiet for four hundred years between the writing of the Old and New Testaments. A God who knows no boundary to space and time. A God who has no use for a microwave, who often seems to act more in the mode of a slow cooker. How do we slow down enough to hear His voice? We have to give Him time. I know that time is a precious commodity for us as humans, but I cannot stress enough that taking and giving time are both necessary as we journey toward finding our joy again and having a real relationship with our Father.

So what did I learn? Get ready for this mind-blowing, life-transforming revelation: faith isn't *just* believing without seeing, and hope *isn't* about what we can accomplish in our own strength. To have, to activate, and to maintain faith, we need to exercise it by taking action. That could be stepping out and believing before we can see the fruits. It could look like confessing with our mouth before we can feel the results. It could even be trusting and believing while in a season of hardship. Faith is stepping out and believing, in confidence, that whatever we ask for in prayer will be granted.

What?! I mean, doesn't that just blow your mind and get you fired up? It's a radical way to look at faith, right? But the truth is that it's biblical! The Bible says in Hebrews 11:1, "Now faith is confidence in what we hope for and assurance about what we do not see." Faith is now. Faith is an action word. Faith is acting upon God's Word. Somehow I had missed those realities for all those years. I had been sitting back and waiting passively for what I was hoping would miraculously appear. I wasn't on my feet with arms extended, reaching out and grabbing onto it, trusting and hoping in God's promises. If this looks like you, it's not too late. Reach out and grab onto this truth and hang on!

So how did Hagin know this? Because he had spent much of his young life in bed, with everyone telling him he was going to die. He had been born with a deformed heart and was believed to have an incurable blood disease. He was not expected to live past the age of 15 and became paralyzed and bedridden. In 1933, after converting to

Christianity, he reported dying three times within ten minutes. He remained paralyzed, but on August 8, 1934, he reports that he was raised from his deathbed after reading Mark 11:23–24 and activating his faith in God's Word:

"For verily I say unto you, That whosoever shall say unto this mountain, Be thou removed and be thou cast into the sea; and shall not doubt in his heart, but shall believe that those things which he saith shall come to pass; he shall have whatsoever he saith. Therefore I say unto you, what things soever ye desire, when ye pray, believe that ye receive them, and ye shall have them."

As Kenneth Hagin read this passage from the King James Version, he believed that he could have the promise of life that God had said was his. He believed what Jesus said in these remarkable verses.

What are *you* wanting to believe today? What are *you* desiring with all of your heart? I would encourage you to step out and believe, in confidence, that whatever you ask for in prayer will be granted to you. When we have this kind of faith, we can find our joy again.

Another key component Kenneth Hagin reveals in *Bible Faith* has to do with our confession. The million-dollar question is what we are openly confessing—out loud—in our lives today. Hagin states, "Faith is measured by our confession. Our usefulness in the Lord is measured by our confession. Sooner or later we become what we confess. There is a confession of our hearts and confession of our lips and when these two harmonize, we become mighty in prayer life. The reason so many are defeated is that they have a negative confession. They talk of their weaknesses and failures and invariably they go down to the level of their confession."

How many times have you walked around saying to yourself, "I'm sick. I'm depressed. I'm angry. I'm confused." I know I have. What snapped me awake was that the words I was declaring—in a very real sense decreeing—were neither lifegiving nor life affirming. If my words don't bring glory to God, who gets their "glory"? Who smirks at them in victory? The enemy! Why would I want to walk around giving glory to the enemy when he has been the one stealing my health, my emotions, and my joy in the first place? I wouldn't, and I don't want to any longer. When I started to understand why words are so important, this made perfect sense. Look with me at the opening verses of Genesis 1:

"In the beginning God created the heavens and the earth. Now the earth was formless and empty, darkness was over the surface of the deep, and the Spirit of God was hovering over the waters. And God said, 'Let there be light,' and there was light. God saw that the light was good, and he separated the light from the darkness. God called the light 'day,' and the darkness he called 'night.' And there was evening, and there was morning—the first day."

What did God do? He spoke. God spoke the world into existence. God's original word was formative, and the words we speak as His image bearers are important, too. What I have described is the God kind of faith. It's the kind of faith I want to have. What about you? To exercise that kind of faith we need to decree not only life-giving words, but specifically God's Word. When the Word of God is in our hearts and lips, we have power over depression, disease, and, yes—over demons—and we can walk victoriously in our life with joy. Amen!

A final thought I took away from Hagin's book is what tied it all together for me. This truth is what we need to remember as we look at the way in which faith and hope will bring us joy. Hagin goes on to say, "Fellowship is the very mother of faith and fellowship is the parent of joy. It is the source of victory. And God has called us individually into fellowship with His Son. If you have fellowship with God and you are walking in the light, as He is in the light, then prayer becomes one of the sweetest and one of the greatest assets to which we have become heirs in Christ."

And doesn't that make sense? The devil's number one goal is to push us out of fellowship with God. He will distract us, lie to us, and isolate us until we are lost and alone, taking advantage of every opportunity to pour lie after lie onto us until we feel as though we are drowning. When we're isolated, alone, flailing around like a rag doll from the storms of life, we will not have joy. Some people continue on this downward path until they are so sad, so lonely, so confused that they just want to end it all. I know. I was there. And maybe you've been there, too.

"The highest honor that the Father has ever conferred upon us is to be 'joint fellow-shippers' with Himself, with His Son, and with the Holy Spirit in carrying out His dreams for the redemption of the human race. But relationship without fellowship is an insipid thing. It is like a marriage relationship without love or fellowship." When I read these words, I feel convicted that Hagin knew exactly what to say to point my eyes to my own relationship with the Lord. Am I in true fellowship with Jesus? Because I knew what it was like to have a marriage that lacked vigor and was without love.

If I am the "church"—the Bride of Christ—having trusted the Lord and received salvation by grace through faith, then I can relate to Paul's words when in 2 Corinthians 11:2 he refers to the church as a virgin waiting for her bridegroom. I can think about how the bride will give her entire self to her husband—mind, body, and soul. Is this a fitting description of my relationship with my Lord—that I am giving Him everything? Or am I giving him only my leftovers each day—my leftover time, energy, and love.

No wonder I went years without laying hold of my true joy and purpose. No wonder I functioned as target practice for the enemy. No wonder I spent years believing every lie. I was missing my one true soul mate, and without fellowship with Him I was lost and alone in the desert of life. But God . . . ! His grace is an endless ocean, and His love extends, much as the arms of Christ were extended on the cross, wide embracing and without end.

There will be times when we don't feel God walking with us. We don't feel His presence with our physical bodies and senses, though we keep hoping with all of *our* strength. But God's Word is still true, and He is still offering promises of life to the fullest, whether or not we have the kind of faith to believe. Again, it comes down to a choice. And I've got to say that I've done it both ways and that now that I know . . . I'll choose Jesus every time. I'm done believing the lies and giving glory to the enemy. I'm done serving Jesus my leftovers. I'm done cooking with a microwave and feeling that if He doesn't answer me within five minutes He's lost interest.

If you're done with all of that, too, let's activate our faith! We've admitted where there was a break in our life and we've laid our baggage down at the foot of the cross. We've unpacked the lies and replaced them with the truth. And now we need to activate our faith and step into that promised land. It may contain giants, but our God is bigger, and we already know how this story ends. Let's cross over—because, Daughter, your faith has healed you. Amen.

Diving Deeper

BREAKOUT

Please use the following pages to answer Chapter 5 questions, take notes, dig deeper, and journal on your journey toward finding joy again.

BREAKOUT QUESTIONS

Please use the space below to write your answers, dig deeper, and journal on your journey toward finding joy again.

Questions to think about, discuss, and answer:

1. What have you been believing about hope and faith?

2. Have your feelings interfered with your faith? If so, which feelings specifically?

3. Examine your relationship with Jesus. In terms of your hopes and expectations, do you envision God as being more like a microwave or more like a slow cooker?

4. What have you been openly confessing in your life? Has your confession been life giving, or are you inadvertently giving glory to the enemy?

5. What are some things you can say, out loud, to decree and declare God's Word?

NOTES

DIVING DEEPER

It may seem challenging to change the way we declare over ourselves and others. But as with anything else that's new to us, we need to use baby steps. You can start by reading verses from the Bible out loud. Instead of saying that you are sick or depressed or naming your perceived diagnosis, you can say:

- "Thank you, Lord, that I walk in divine health."
- "Thank you, Lord, that You are my joy!"
- "Thank you, Lord, that you are my peace."

Decree and declare what you believe. Go back to your foundation—decreeing and declaring what you *know* to be true, as well as who you really are in Jesus Christ.

All of us are going to make mistakes. We are going to sin, and the enemy will try to pull us away from God, His fellowship, and His forgiveness. But we can declare aloud something that Kenneth Hagin wrote for just such an occasion:

"Yes, that's right Mr. Devil—I did that and I was wrong. But, 1 John 1:9 says that if I confess my sin, God is faithful and just to forgive me and to cleanse me from all unrighteousness. So . . . God has forgiven me and I'm thanking Him for it." Now go away!!

PRAYER

Father God, Lord Jesus, Holy Spirit,

Thank You! Thank You for speaking only life-giving words. Thank You for Your Word. Keep pointing me there to receive Your truth. Forgive me when I've given you my leftovers. I want to be in relationship with You. I want to give you everything I have because You have given everything for me. I love You and am ready to cross over into Your promised land. I'm ready for everything You have for me. I choose YOU! Help me to decree and declare only Your goodness and truth over myself and others. I want to activate my faith. I want my JOY, the kind that only You can give. I ask all of these things in the mighty name of Jesus. Amen.

JOURNAL

CHAPTER 6

Daughter, Your Faith Has Healed You

*I*f you looked at the front inside page, you noticed that I dedicated this book to Marj Newhouse. She was a divine connection I met at a ministry banquet. There was just something that drew us to each other to share our stories. That's what divine connection is all about. At the end of the banquet, we talked briefly and compared ministries and stories, and I told her about my first book, *In Over My Head*. She bought and read it, and we continued to stay in touch. Later on I learned that Marj had two grandchildren—one who worked in the emergency room of a local hospital and the other who was a police officer for a local city.

Marj was troubled by their stories of meeting people who were without hope. While these individuals remained nameless, and their stories didn't delineate detail, the common denominator was the sheer number of people who tried to end their lives. I remember the day I received a message from her: "I've been thinking about doing a class to help those struggling with depression. I've read your story. Would you consider teaching?"

We were just about to start a vacation, so I told her I would pray about it and get back to her. On the way home the following week, it was as though God downloaded the title of the class, that the material needed to cover five weeks in length, and what the topic of each week would be. I reached out to Marj, and she was dumbfounded. Our journey of joy had begun.

I had never taught a class before. Sure, I'd led Bible studies and spoken in front of large groups, but this was different—I needed to write the curriculum. But not only that, we needed to set up the class, create a registration process, and put the word out there. Who would come to such a class? What would it look like? Were there people out there trying to find their joy again? I kept stepping out in faith.

We set the dates for the first five-week class, and the countdown began. I started advertising on Facebook and on JOY 99—a local radio station—and we told everyone we knew. Between the radio ads and Facebook, women started to register for the class, and we had a morning and evening roster. It was ALL God, and it was truly amazing to watch Him work. I continued to prepare and write out the notes for the first week so I would be ready, but that's all I had.

The first week came and went, and it was incredible to see the need for joy being met. God had made it clear that what we needed was His full armor and that we were living in the midst of a battle, even though most of us didn't even know it. Each week I would write out the notes for the next Tuesday, and He would give me the material one week at a time. I had the outline, but the meat and potatoes came like manna from heaven—as though I were waiting on God for each meal. It was only when we got to the fifth and final week, and I was recapping what we had learned to date, that the full picture was revealed.

As I said, we started the class talking about the full armor of God:

- The Belt of Truth (truth is the belt that holds all the other pieces of armor in place).
- The Breastplate of Righteousness (covers the heart and shields it and the other vital organs).
- Shoes of the Gospel (Ladies, our favorite accessory!). We must put on gospel shoes that will allow us to march wherever the Lord leads.
- Shield of Faith (Paul says, "In addition to all this, take up the shield of faith, with which you can extinguish all the flaming arrows of the evil one" (Ephesians 6:16).
- Helmet of Salvation (the helmet protects the head—perhaps the most vital part of the body since it is the seat of thought and the housing of the mind).

- Sword of the Spirit (the only weapon of offense in the armor of God. All the other parts are defensive. God's Word is described as "alive and active" and "sharper than any double-edged sword" (Hebrews 4:12).
- And finally, prayer: "Pray in the Spirit on all occasions with all kinds of prayers and requests" (Ephesians 6:18). Even when you are clothed with the armor of God, you need to bathe it all in prayer.

As I was writing all of this out, the Holy Spirit reminded me that over the last four weeks of the class we had just been practicing putting on the armor and learning what each piece felt like. In week one we had established our foundation: we believe in Christ, including His sacrificial death for our sins; we ended that class asking for forgiveness and recognizing that we are nothing without Him. At the next session we had picked up the Breastplate of Righteousness, acknowledging that it is Christ's righteousness and not our own that covers us. In week three we had worked on putting on the Belt of Truth by going to God's Word to replace our lies with His truth. In week four we had talked about how, now that we knew the truth, we were going to pass that truth on to others. Were we going to allow the Lord to use our stories to help others? We had all been commissioned to march wherever He leads and spread the gospel of Christ. We tried on those shoes of the gospel and agreed that they felt pretty good.

On week four we had also picked up that Shield of Faith as we learned that faith and hope bring joy. And as we are in fellowship with Him, that faith grows from a mustard seed size to an entire field of beautiful yellow flowers, protecting us and allowing us to live a victorious life in Christ.

At the session for week two we had learned about the lies we believe and how important it is for us to put on the Helmet of Salvation. When we are confident of our salvation, believing the truth in what God says about us, we will not be moved by Satan's deceptions.

In weeks three and four we had learned how powerful God's Word is in our life, and why it is so important that we study the Bible and become familiar with its truth and power. The Sword of the Spirt—God's Word—both protects us and destroys our enemy, the devil, and his temptations.

Each week we had been praying—praying over the classes and praying for each other. This is how we do battle and how we fellowship with God. How do we keep our joy? We put on the full armor of God. Each piece is important and necessary for us to live effectively in this world.

When I got done writing out all of the notes for the fifth class, I was simply awe-struck that the Lord would bring me—and, in turn, us—full circle to understand the importance of His armor and the imperative not only of finding but also of *keeping* our joy. I believed that the reason His message had come weekly was that I myself was still in a learning mode. He had been unfolding His truth in a way that I could internalize, claim, and integrate, in a way that would allow that truth to become a part of me.

But there was one final lesson He wanted to impart to His children. As I continued to write out my notes, the Holy Spirit whispered that the week five class needed to be all about how we activate our faith. I had just read about this in Kenneth Hagin's *Bible Faith*, and it had touched me deeply. This was something everyone needed to know.

To do this now, let's read Mark 5:24–34 together. Hagin points out to the reader that we can have whatever we are asking for—in this case, our joy—when we do the four things this woman did in the verses below:

> So Jesus went with him.
>
> A large crowd followed and pressed around him. And a woman was there who had been subject to bleeding for twelve years. She had suffered a great deal under the care of many doctors and had spent all she had, yet instead of getting better she grew worse. When she heard about Jesus, she came up behind him in the crowd and touched his cloak, because she thought, "If I just touch his clothes, I will be healed." Immediately her bleeding stopped and she felt in her body that she was freed from her suffering.
>
> At once Jesus realized that power had gone out from him. He turned around in the crowd and asked, "Who touched my clothes?"

"You see the people crowding against you," his disciples answered, "and yet you can ask, 'Who touched me?'"

But Jesus kept looking around to see who had done it. Then the woman, knowing what had happened to her, came and fell at his feet and, trembling with fear, told him the whole truth. He said to her, "Daughter, your faith has healed you. Go in peace and be freed from your suffering."

This is an amazing story of faith and healing. So let's look at the four steps Hagin was referring to:

Step #1 Say it

What is the first step this woman took in order to receive from Jesus? Verse 28 records her thought process: "If I just touch his clothes, I will be healed." The first step she took was to say it. In the last chapter, we asked ourselves these questions: What are we openly confessing in our lives? What are we decreeing and declaring? We should never speak defeat. If we are called believers, then we need to believe.

Step #2 Do it

The woman followed through on her recognition of the truth. She came up behind Jesus in the crowd and touched His cloak. Can you imagine her great desire to be healed? She had been bleeding for 12 years, probably living separately from her friends and family because she was considered unclean. But she risked everything because she believed. And she stepped out in that belief.

Step #3 Receive it

Verse 29 reads: "Immediately her bleeding stopped and she felt in her body that she was freed from her suffering." She received His healing and immediately felt the change in her body. Hagin writes, "notice that the feeling and the healing followed the saying and doing." As we discussed in the last chapter, to spark our faith we need to take action. That could be stepping out and believing before we can see the fruits. She stepped out, believing that Jesus would heal her. She touched his cloak, and she was healed. Praise God!

Step #4 Tell it

Verse 33 reads, "Then the woman, knowing what had happened to her, came and fell at his feet and, trembling with fear, told him the whole truth." We need to tell it, too, my friends. Our testimony is a powerful weapon that not only gives God glory but lets others see what Jesus has done in our lives. You not only need to say it and do it, but you need to receive it and tell it. Amen.

This isn't the only example of the four steps found in the Bible. Let's look at two others. Turn with me to 1 Samuel 17 and read verses 1–11 and 34–54. Once you've read those passages, let's talk about David and Goliath.

What four things did David do?

1. David said he would go and kill Goliath.
2. David went and knocked Goliath down with his sling and stone.
3. David then took Goliath's own sword and cut off his head, killing him.
4. David then told the story to everyone by taking Goliath's head to Jerusalem and putting Goliath's weapons in his own tent.

What I love about this story is how the writer allows the entire provocation to unfold. We hear Goliath taunting the Israelites. We see David trying on the king's armor. We listen to David telling King Saul that God has trained him for just such a job. We see David walk out to the line and doing something only God could have orchestrated. Isn't that indicative of our lives? There will be giants we need to fight. We will be the only ones for the job. And God has been preparing us for battle. He is doing so even now.

Let's look at one more example. Read Luke 15:11–32.

This is the classic story of the prodigal (or lost) son. I can easily insert myself into these verses and look back at the times I've walked away from God. But just like this earthly father, God celebrates when we return. What are the four things the son did?

1. First, he said, "I will set out and go back to my father and say to him: Father, I have sinned against heaven and against you. I am no longer worthy to be called your son."
2. He did it. He started down the road toward home.
3. He received forgiveness, reconciliation, and welcome. The son was reunited with his father and received his inheritance as son.
4. The Father of the lost son told it: "We had to celebrate and be glad, because this brother of yours was dead and is alive again; he was lost and is found."

Aren't these incredible stories of activating faith? I would encourage you as you meditate on God's Word to look for other areas in the Bible where these four steps are literally walked out. But examples of this aren't limited to the Bible. These four steps work today. I told you about how *Finding Joy Again* got started. What was once a dream was spoken out loud. We trusted God, stepped out, and started to put things in motion, believing that God would be faithful. Already on that first day of classes we received the full measure of God's faithfulness and could tangibly see how he was orchestrating everything. And now . . . well, I've been telling this story over and over again.

But there's more than just the classes; it's the conference and the book and everything He wants to do from here. When He gives us a dream, the only way we can step into that reality is by deliberately stepping out. Now that I'm here in the promised land, I want to receive every gift and every promise and engage in every adventure. What about you? Remember, to solidify faith we need to take action. That could be stepping out and believing before we can see the fruits. That could be confessing with our mouth before feeling the results. It could even be trusting and believing while in a season of hardship. Faith is stepping out and believing, in confidence, that whatever we ask for in prayer will be granted to us.

Daughter, your *faith* has healed you. Let those words wash over you today. Take this moment to bask in His love and receive every good gift He wants to give you. Take the four steps . . . go ahead and step out. Stay on this journey of JOY and know in your heart of hearts that it is yours for the taking.

Diving Deeper

BREAKOUT

Please use the following pages to answer Chapter 6 questions, take notes, dig deeper, and journal on your journey toward finding joy again.

BREAKOUT QUESTIONS

Please use the space below to write your answers, dig deeper, and journal on your journey toward finding joy again.

Questions to think about, discuss, and answer:

1. Have you ever heard of Kenneth Hagin's four steps before?

2. Can you find other stories in the Bible that reflect these four steps?

3. Do you see in your own life instances in which you took those four steps, maybe without even realizing it?

4. What giants in your life are stopping you from experiencing this God kind of faith?

5. Is God revealing a dream inside you? Are you ready to step out and turn it into reality?

NOTES

DIVING DEEPER

I have found that it is in the most difficult situations that we long to have faith. We cry out to God, some of us for the first time, in the hallways of the hospital or alongside the road after an accident. We search for Him in the smoke-filled rooms of a house engulfed in flames or standing beside the grave of someone we love. I've seen the criminal cry out to God while stuck in a store he had tried to rob, after failing to find his way out. Over and over he cried out His name, having exhausted all other means and giving in to his fate.

When I see this time and time again, it makes me wonder how people can believe there is no God or that they can live without Him—when eventually we all cry out to Him. We don't often feel a need for Him when life is moving smoothly and everything seems to be going our way. Then the faith we have is in ourselves. But when things start to spin out of control, we humans recognize that our own "control" is really an illusion . . . and we instinctively cry out to our Creator.

But what if we were to reach for God, not only in the hard times but all the time? What if we were to start believing that we were created for a purpose, that God loves us, and that He sent His Son to give us the gift of everlasting life? All we have to do is reach out our hand and take it. All we have to do is trust in the promises of

His Word and open the door to our hearts. All we have to do is have faith as tiny as a mustard seed, and we can move mountains. Do you believe? Do you have faith?

PRAYER

Father God, Lord Jesus, Holy Spirit,

I'll admit, there have been many times in my life when I haven't had faith. I've struggled with the lies from the enemy and didn't believe You were big enough. But I know now that wasn't true. I want to have a God kind of faith. I want to receive all that You have in store for me. Forgive me, Lord. Renew my mind and grow my faith in You. Help me to step out and believe before I see the fruits. Help me to confess with my mouth before I see the results. I'm activating my faith, Lord. I believe. I ask all of these things in the mighty name of Jesus. Amen.

JOURNAL

CHAPTER 7

Find the JOY

*I*t's easy to get caught up in all the negative things going on in this world. After a long day at school or work or taking care of your children or grandchildren, watching sixty minutes of your local and world news can solidify all the negative things you felt throughout the day. You may feel bombarded, as though you've been struggling all day with your nose reaching just above the surface of a tank of water, on your tiptoes, no less—and now, watching the TV, you've been pushed down below the surface and can no longer be seen.

Are we fighting a losing battle? Maybe, just maybe, we are focusing on the wrong things. One producer's view of a news story is not the only perspective. A magazine cover with pictures of distraught couples fighting is not the only version. Images on Facebook and other social media outlets are not the only truth. We have to be a vigilant participants in looking for our truth in this world—especially for where to find our joy. Because when we focus on the wrong things, we're traveling down a road that is challenging in terms of finding our way back.

In my case, I spent years focusing on the wrong things. For one, I focused on myself. I was so wrapped up in my own pain, my own troubles, my own sadness—that I couldn't see the struggle in others. Each day I lay under my own pain, covered up in my despair as though under a heavy blanket, wrapping myself up and wanting to never leave. This is where the enemy wants us to stay. When we're focused on ourselves, for good or bad, we can't see others . . . and we can't be used by God. When we're focused on ourselves and stuck in these painful moments, we're not activating our faith, and we're not believing all of God's promises.

What I needed to do was lift my eyes and focus on Jesus. The Bible gives us hope when we read verses like these:

> "I press on toward the goal to win the prize for which God has called me heavenward in Christ Jesus" (Philippians 3:14).

> "I lift up my eyes to the mountains—where does my help come from? My help comes from the LORD, the Maker of heaven and earth" (Psalm 121:1–2).

> "Lift up your eyes and look to the heavens: Who created all these? He who brings out the starry host one by one and calls forth each of them by name.

Because of his great power and mighty strength, not one of them is missing" (Isaiah 40:26).

I believe that we lose our joy when we don't focus on Jesus, when we look at this world only with our physical eyes. We get wrapped up in how the world looks from our limited vantage point, and we can't reconcile in our minds how an all-powerful God could let there be struggle, pain, sickness, hunger, death, and the kind of devastation that is tangible and metastasizing. What we're not remembering is that the way things are right now was not His original plan. If you want proof of that, go to Genesis and read chapters 1–3. You'll read about how God spoke our world into existence and gave us a beautiful creation to live in. He made us in His image, gave us the world to rule over, and moved among us freely—walking and talking in relationship and love.

But then the whisper . . . The enemy of our soul arrives on the scene and speaks to Eve in the garden: "Did God really say, 'You must not eat from any tree in the garden?'. . . You will not certainly die, . . . for God knows that when you eat from it your eyes will be opened, and you will be like God, knowing good and evil" (Genesis 3:1, 4–5).

Aren't those the words we're still hearing today? "Did God *really* say: you are forgiven? You are healed? You are loved? You are worthy? You have your joy?" But God . . . ! In His infinite love for us, He started this world down a path of restoration. When we failed by listening to the enemy, God orchestrated a way of redemption, sending His only Son to walk among us, restore us to Himself, and break the curse of sin and death that came the day Eve listened to those words and tasted the fruit in the garden.

When we look at this world with our physical eyes without focusing on Jesus, we see the effects of the curse. We see the perpetual motion of the earth that has been dying a slow death. We as Christians have a front row seat to see the enemy's window of opportunity closing; he is doing everything he can to distract us from God in these final days. We are looking at this world as the end, as though this is all there is. We lose our joy when we look at this world as it is now.

What we should be focusing on is our true home in heaven. What we should be focusing on are the promises of God and the restoration He is enacting even now:

> The desert and the parched land will be glad;
>> the wilderness will rejoice and blossom.
> Like the crocus, it will burst into bloom;
>> it will rejoice greatly and shout for joy.
> The glory of Lebanon will be given to it,
>> the splendor of Carmel and Sharon;
> they will see the glory of the LORD,
>> the splendor of our God.

Strengthen the feeble hands,
    steady the knees that give way;
say to those with fearful hearts,
    "Be strong, do not fear;
your God will come,
    he will come with vengeance;
with divine retribution
    he will come to save you."

Then will the eyes of the blind be opened
    and the ears of the deaf unstopped.
Then will the lame leap like a deer,
    and the mute tongue shout for joy.
Water will gush forth in the wilderness
    and streams in the desert.
The burning sand will become a pool,
    the thirsty ground bubbling springs.
In the haunts where jackals once lay,
    grass and reeds and papyrus will grow.

And a highway will be there;
    it will be called the Way of Holiness;
    it will be for those who walk on that Way.
The unclean will not journey on it;
    wicked fools will not go about on it.
No lion will be there,
    nor any ravenous beast;
    they will not be found there.

But only the redeemed will walk there,
> and those the LORD has rescued will return.
They will enter Zion with singing;
> everlasting joy will crown their heads.
Gladness and joy will overtake them,
> and sorrow and sighing will flee away.
> (Isaiah 35:1–10)

This was written seven hundred years before Jesus was born. The people were waiting for their Messiah and knew without a doubt that when He arrived His appearance would change everything. Now we are waiting for Him to come again, trusting and believing that when He returns we will be ushered into our eternal home. We need to remember that, while we are on different journeys, we have but one destination in view: heaven. This life is only a blip on the radar compared to an eternity in heaven with Jesus. When we lift our heads and focus not with our physical eyes but with our spirits, trusting in the Holy Spirit and in God's promises, we can see that this world is only temporary and that "our present troubles are small and won't last very long. Yet they produce for us a glory that vastly outweighs them and will last forever!" (2 Corinthians 4:17 NLT).

When I finally lifted my head and looked to Jesus, I could see that I wasn't the only one struggling. After Jesus healed me, He invited me to Guatemala in August 2015 and showed me what it was like to lift my eyes to see and serve the hurting and the lost. Traveling the bustling streets, buzzing with multitudes of people, scattered with trash and abandoned metal carcasses that were once vehicles, my eyes were opened to another world. Metal shacks peppered the colorful hillsides as the roads weaved and climbed the mountainous terrain we traveled. When we finally arrived at the village, we were greeted by young and old alike, decked out in their best clothes, eager to pray over us and share everything they had.

Over the next seven days, we would be building homes and conducting a vacation Bible school at the community church. We would be giving preselected families new homes: small steel buildings that would hold generations. But I would gain the most from this life-altering opportunity to function as His hands and feet. I would walk away forever changed with a commission to serve the lost, the broken, the hungry, and the forgotten. I would serve those who were like me.

I was reminded that we've all been commissioned; I invite you to read the words of Jesus recorded in Matthew 25:35–40:

> "For I was hungry and you gave me something to eat, I was thirsty and you gave me something to drink, I was a stranger and you invited me in, I needed clothes and you clothed me, I was sick and you looked after me, I was in prison and you came to visit me."

Then the righteous will answer him, "Lord, when did we see you hungry and feed you, or thirsty and give you something to drink? When did we see you a stranger and invite you in, or needing clothes and clothe you? When did we see you sick or in prison and go to visit you?" The King will reply, "Truly I tell you, whatever you did for one of the least of these brothers and sisters of mine, you did for me."

When we read these verses, we realize not only that we're commissioned to help those in need but that we're not the only ones struggling and fighting. While living on this earth we're fighting a battle, and it's not just us but *all* our brothers and sisters in Christ around the world. We read in 1 Peter 5:8–11:

Be alert and of sober mind. Your enemy the devil prowls around like a roaring lion looking for someone to devour. Resist him, standing firm in the faith, because you know that the family of believers throughout the world is undergoing the same kind of sufferings.

And the God of all grace, who called you to his eternal glory in Christ, and you have suffered a little while, will himself restore you and make you strong, firm and steadfast. To him be the power for ever and ever. Amen.

As these verses state, our family of believers is not just inside our home or in our backyard but throughout the world. When we put on the full armor of Christ, we're not only fighting for ourselves but for everyone else. This is a great responsibility and a better focus than just what's happening in our *own* "world." When I realized this, my troubles seemed to diminish in comparison to the issues I could see all around me. My perspective changed, and feeling sorry for myself was no longer an option.

When I finally looked at Jesus *and* others, I could see *myself* more clearly. I could see that true beauty was the way God painted the sky at the start of each new day. I could see His hands in the new life of my granddaughter and in how she quieted when brought up to the crook of her mother's neck. I could see the love in each expression of kindness God prompted me to do, whether handing steaming coffee to a stranger or hugging someone who needed to feel God's love through my embrace.

I now stood in front of the mirror of my life and saw myself the way God saw me: as the daughter of the Most High King. She was no longer weighted down by the baggage of her life and the mistakes she had made but stood on the promises of His Word, assured that He had a purpose and plan for her life. She had replaced each lie with the truth, activated her faith, and finally found her joy.

And that is precisely where you will find it. Not in the world in seeking approval from others, not in rating and measuring your happiness using a scale based on your past pain and heartache. You'll find your joy when you look to Jesus, the author of our restoration and rebirth. When you lift your head and seek His face, His truth, and His love. You'll find your joy when you see **o**thers' needs and realize how you can function as His hands and feet. And you'll find your joy when you see **y**ourself the way God sees you—as the child of the Most High King. **JOY!**

It's easy to get caught up in all of the negative things of this world, my friends. It's easy to lose our joy. But when we stay awake and alert, focusing on Jesus, putting on the full armor of God and fighting the battle . . . we will win every time. And when you forget—and you will—you just need to return. Get out that GPS and start reading your truth. Remain in His love, and before you know it you'll be traveling longer distances, luggage free and picking up that sword more and more often. This is a journey. And never forget that Jesus is walking with you. He doesn't promise that it will be easy . . . but He does promise that He'll never leave your side.

When I look back at my life and what I've gone through, I realize I wouldn't change a thing. Sure, I have regret. I've made plenty of mistakes, traveled down the wrong roads, made poor choices, and hurt the people around me. But if I hadn't done those things, walking through each lesson that God showed me, I wouldn't be who I am today. I wouldn't have the appreciation I enjoy for the peaceful seasons, and the seasons when I have plenty, because I've been through the storm and have lived without. I wouldn't know the true meaning of joy because I've struggled with depression and have slept beneath the heavy blanket of despair. I am what I am today because of my journey . . . AND the faithfulness of a Father who loves me and has never let go of my hand.

I may have spent the first three-quarters of my life trying to make a good first impression. I may have thought those first thirty seconds were imperative for me. I may have felt a need for that person to believe that I was healthy. To believe that I was perfect. To believe that I had it altogether. To believe that I was happy. But I plan on spending my remaining days sharing *this* good news: I am the daughter of the Most High King. I have put on my shoes of the gospel and am marching to a town near you, proclaiming His truth and His joy. I pray that after reading this book you will do the same.

But that question—the one I asked and answered so many times in years past—is still hanging out there today: How are *you*? I pray that this journey has taken you to the point at which you can truly answer. I pray that you've taken off the "I'm fine" shirt and are walking a path of truth. I pray that you've laid your baggage at the foot of the cross and are finally free. I pray that you've replaced the lies with the truth and have activated your faith. I pray that you have finally found *your* joy again and will never again question your identity in Christ!

March on, my friends, and until we meet again I pray God's richest blessings on your lives. Amen.

"As the Father has loved me, so have I loved you. Now remain in my love. If you keep my commands, you will remain in my love, just as I have kept my Father's commands and remain in his love. I have told you this so that my joy may be in you and that your joy may be complete."

— JOHN 15:9–11

Diving Deeper

BREAKOUT

Please use the following pages to answer Chapter 7 questions, take notes, dig deeper, and journal on your journey toward finding joy again.

BREAKOUT QUESTIONS

Please use the space below to write your answers, dig deeper, and journal on your journey toward finding joy again.

Questions to think about, discuss, and answer:

1. Do you get caught up in the negative things of this world?

2. What, specifically, do you fear?

3. Do you see this life as a blip on the radar, or do you have a hard time believing there is more?

4. What are some ways in which you can stop thinking about yourself and your current situation and focus on others?

5. After reading this book, what do you feel you still need to work on? What are you still struggling with to find your joy?

NOTES

DIVING DEEPER

When Paul wrote Philippians, he was sitting in a prison in Rome. Paul knew it wasn't about the situation he was in; it was about the work Jesus was doing in and through him in that season of his life. We have all been in some kind of prison: a prisoner of a situation, a lifestyle, an addiction— even a prisoner of our mind. But we need to have hope and faith that God is not finished with us yet. Let Him finish the work that He has begun in you. He will break your chains and give you the kind of freedom that can be found only in Him, as well as the prize of everlasting life.

> Not that I have already obtained all this, or have already arrived at my goal, but I press on to take hold of that for which Christ Jesus took hold of me. Brothers and Sisters, I do not consider myself yet to have taken hold of it. But one thing I do: Forgetting what is behind me and straining toward what is ahead, I press on toward the goal to win the prize for which God has called me heavenward in Christ Jesus. (Philippians 3:12–14)

PRAYER

Father God, Lord Jesus, Holy Spirit,

It has been an incredible journey. Thank You walking with me each step of the way and speaking to my heart. I am ready to live a life that is filled with Your joy. I am ready to stand on Your promises and know Your truth. I am ready to follow wherever You lead me. Help me, Lord, to each day put on the full armor of God and do battle. Help me to war not only for myself but for my family and friends and those I do not know. Help me to be Your hands and feet and to share Your love with everyone I meet. I love You. Lord. Thank You for loving me. Amen.

JOURNAL

Acknowledgments

I wish to express my sincerest thanks to my family and friends, who have encouraged me not only to write but to step out in faith and conduct my first national conference. To all of the ladies who have already taken the five-week class or will do so in the future, I pray that this book will be as much a blessing to you as you have been to me. We will forever be sisters in Christ. To Jeanne, my mentor, who has journeyed with me, listening to the Holy Spirit's revelation and provision of the next thing I would need. To my husband, Kurt, who has not only watched me step off the cliff and into God's loving hands but has stepped with me. Thank you for your devotion and support. I love you and am so glad God chose you for me. But most importantly to MY beloved, my God. Thank you for always showing up, always whispering to my heart of hearts, always answering every prayer. I love you with an everlasting love. Thank you for helping me find *my* joy again . . . in You!

Notes

"As the Father has loved me, so have I loved you.
Now remain in my love."

—JOHN 15:9